Sacred Cows

Fay
WELDON

Sacred Cows

Chatto & Windus
LONDON

Published in 1989 by
Chatto & Windus Ltd
30 Bedford Square
London WC1B 3SG

A CIP catalogue record for this book
is available from the British Library

ISBN 0 7011 3556 5

Photoset in Linotron Ehrhardt by
Rowland Phototypesetting Ltd
Bury St Edmunds, Suffolk
Printed in Great Britain by
Redwood Burn Ltd
Trowbridge, Wiltshire

Prologue

A parable
And while the wedding feast waited the woman
took weevily meal and brackish water and set them
in a cracked bowl and there was no good in them.
Then she added yeast and sour milk and because
the yeast was as manna the dough rose and she
baked it in a good oven and when it was cooked it
was divided into parts and there was much nourishment in it and rejoicing at the wedding feast.

The interpretation (or reading, as they say down here
in the mystic West Country, home of tarot cards,
the *I Ching*, astrological charts and the like. The
Witch of Endor rides her broomstick in full daylight
around these parts, and is extending her dominions
East and North, and the Church doesn't utter a
squeak, but that's another matter).

For 'weevily meal' read wholemeal flour, the stuff
of self-congratulation. 'My diet is natural so my

I

conscience is clear.' We have thought about our bodies too much and the society we live in too little.

For 'brackish water' read tap-water, symbol of our apathy. London water is rich in oestrogen; it comes from the urine of the women in Reading, where the birth pill's popular (a matter, surely, for philosophical discourse, rich in physiological implication, but our only response is 'down with privatisation!').

The 'cracked bowl' is the cowardice the past engenders. We take lessons from history that we shouldn't. 'Can't do that!' we say. 'Look what happened last time.' But now is never quite the same as then.

Who'd have thought you could make anything from beginnings so lamentable? But then –

The yeast works in the sour milk: Salman Rushdie pulls his rich fermenting images down from the sky and drops them into the milk (the usual lukewarm mixture of bile and good intentions mixed) and it begins to foam and fizz in the most terrifying way

– *And the oven is good* – that is to say the time is ripe; things simply can't go on as they are, or we will *all* be rioting in the streets crying kill, kill, kill

– and the bread was divided and there was nourishment in it – if we work for a just society (forget the mealy-mouthing chatter of a 'caring' society: we 'care' more than you do, do, don't, do, don't) we might just, still, bring all the ingredients together in triumphant success – *and then there will indeed be rejoicing at the wedding feast.*

But first, I suspect, 'active citizens' all, we must put on sackcloth for a time, and smear ourselves with ashes, and repent of our various follies and self-deceptions, or we'll get nowhere. Not even the yeast will save us.

◇

Sackcloth and Ashes

THE RUSHDIE AFFAIR swept over Britain like a tidal wave and, receding, left us stripped of a few more illusions, our self-esteem more tattered than ever, fit for nothing. 'Speak for yourself!' you may say.

I do, I do.

I repent my past attitudes, the ill-founded assumptions I had, the idle and mischievous suppositions I toyed with, the easy intellectual options sired by paranoia out of wishful thinking which I chose: I mourn lost opportunities; I grieve for hopes abandoned. And I want (as ever) not to be alone: I want to be agreed with, which is why I write. I want you to wear sackcloth and ashes too. It is hard to stand alone, looking dusty and dirty.

Please understand this 'I' is fictional. The one I speak of, currently putting on sackcloth and ashes, the garb of the penitent, is a familiar leftish humanist feminist, of the kind who've been trying to shove the world along but doing it from the wrong direction and therefore to no avail – a little figure you see in a computer game kicking and shoving and wildly flailing against an invisible wall, just the other side of which is a stool, which if you could only move you could leap upon (shift key, please) and be out the door to meet a fresh set of new and exciting challenges.

I hope you are acquainted with computer games: those containable patterns of challenge and change. (No wonder they fascinate the young: perpetual parables that they are. If this, then that. If that, then this.) But I bet you, the reader of a Chatto & Windus 10,000-word broadsheet, are above them: you think computer games are for the mindless. If so, you cut yourself off from great pleasure. Bet you haven't read the Koran either. Nor me, until the tidal wave swept it up directly in front of me, and there it was, unavoidable – this wildly prophetic, wonderful poem, this revelation from Allah to Mohammed in the sixth century, this set of rigid rules for living, perceiving and thinking. Now the penalties for doubt and disobedience laid down by the Koran are extreme: that is to say the fires of Gehenna wait, and burn fiercely and painfully for anyone who dares to argue, or say 'hold on a moment, are you *sure*?' Chastisement for non-belief is plentiful and extreme. Just open it to read, and your peace of mind has gone. Booby-trapped! Supposing it's true? 'Allah is all-forgiving, all compassionate' goes the nervous refrain, but what, I ask myself, does Allah have to *forgive*? What has this dreadful Lord of Vengeance got to be compassionate *about*? He invents the sin if only to be seen as kindly in excusing it. It is a circular argument, puzzling to Western ears.

The Bible, in its entirety, is at least food for thought. The Koran is food for no-thought. It is not a poem on which a society can be safely or sensibly based. It forbids change, interpretation, self-knowledge or even art, for fear of treading on Allah's creative toes. My novels don't sell in Muslim countries. My particular parables, my alternative realities, don't suit. How could they, being the works of an unclean female unbeliever? Though if we are to trust the Koran, women (believers, that is) do get to heaven. They do have souls. That's something! But since heaven is a place where men delight themselves with virgin houris, with glasses of wine beneath the bough, it's hard to see what the grown women do there. Fetch the wine and wash the glasses, I expect.

It is easy to mock other people's religions. They're all absurd, at one level. So's Christianity. What, sits on the right side, does He? Not the left? Mockery is valuable, if only to define belief. Language fails to express the ineffable: perhaps that's why we work so hard at it. Words can only ever be approximate, mere stabs at meaning, agreed upon by a consensus to stand for this and that. Allah, Jehovah, the Trinity. The Koran fails in that being so abusive of non-belief it insists upon a concrete interpretation of its text. Thus it gives weapons and strength to the thought police – and the thought police are easily set marching, and they frighten.

Sackcloth and ashes, that so few of us bothered to read the Koran; but instead murmured platitudes about 'great world religions' and thought Iran and Iraq were far-off places, whose troubles had nothing to do with us, and smiled amiably but without comprehension at the wild-eyed Iranians in our city streets who handed out their desperate leaflets, tales of imprisonment, torture and war. The world has got very small, too small for us to ignore.

Sackcloth and ashes that, taken up by our preoccupation with the evils of 'Thatcherism', the trivia of our party-political moans and groans, rocking gently to the familiar lullaby of paranoia and apathy mixed, we sleep: the sharp crack of an airliner exploding makes us stir a little, but we soon sink back, blaming the Minister of Transport as we close our eyes. Only the mad bombers again. Let them tighten up security. Nightie-night. Then comes the murmur of 'kill, kill, kill' from our own backstreets, and the crackle of

7

pages burning, and that disturbs a few of us, and an eye or two reluctantly opens, and a polite letter or so appears in the newspapers, and a few more read the Rushdie book. Fellow's on their side, it seems – on Camden's Race Relations Board even – doesn't like the police much, does he – what's all this about Mohammed and Gileel, Angel and Devil, Good and Evil both together in the same place, the wrong one sprouting horns, the other growing wings: falling to earth? Bit Manichean, what – you know, the heresy; that the God who permits evil *is* evil – well, okay, we all know that over here, don't we, in the heart of civilisation, the focus of European culture: its growth point: go to a concert at the Festival Hall and you pass through Cardboard City: obvious. Fellow can write, can't deny it: all those words splashed over the page: words you never thought of: everything mixed, not just Good and Evil, but the mandarin and the colloquial, the profound and the trivial, sacred and profane, the appalling and the hilarious, past and present all mixed up – police vans and butterfly crusades – what is he trying to *do*? Make one world of us, one creation of us? And why are these primitive folk up North, these mad fundamentalists, these people who believe words are magic, why are they carrying on like this? Do they really believe God is *good*, and that's all there is to it? Trying to kill the messenger of bad news, the one saying God is not good? They must be insane. God isn't good. Look around.

Like being back in the middle ages perhaps – like the witch-burnings. Could it be? Someone had to be responsible for the bad things going on – disease, impotent men, barren women, crop failure – so blame the witches. Just as God has to have saints to mediate between heaven and earth, so Satan has to have witches to mediate between hell and earth. Well, things have to be fair. Ask any child.

So that's it. They're burning *The Satanic Verses* as once witches were burned: to keep the world safe. A bit drastic, but we see their point.

Their hearts are in the right place – it's just they're a bit primitive. Well, Arabs. Pakis. Muslims. All the same.

Come to think of it, they're probably on the verge of losing their faith: they'd have to be, living in this advanced and intelligent society of ours: that's why there's this sudden outburst. Last throes of a daft religion. Goodnight.

A Fatah from the Ayatollah, the despatching of death squads after one of our own. A jolt. Eyes fly open. People sit up. This is *serious*.

Please let us not go to sleep again.

◇

Kill, Kill, Kill

SACKCLOTH AND ashes, that we no longer ask ourselves what we mean, but create a cliché at the drop of a hat, at the sweep back to sea of the tidal wave. How easily the 'deep hurt of the Muslim community' came to the lips, as explanation and justification of rioting in the streets, book-burning, threats and intimidation. A hurt so deep it could only be eased by the death of the one who caused it? 'Deep hurt' like 'Deep Heat' – the rheumatic's favourite ointment – becoming almost one word, so often it was spoken. But *what* was deeply hurt? Self-esteem? Belief? Mohammed? Allah himself? How could someone's death ease it? Death is not an ointment, merely another exacerbation. What sort of excuse for barbarity is this 'deep hurt'? But still the phrase was uttered in hushed and reverential tones by atheist, agnostic and believer alike.

> Hush, hush, whisper who dares,
> Christopher Robin is saying his prayers.

And if the prayer is kill, kill, kill, the Koran says so, too bad. Mind you, when Muslims say 'Rushdie should die' they often add 'though of course I wouldn't do it myself' – in much the same spirit as women will say 'I'm not a feminist, though of course I do believe in equal pay, equal rights, equal dignity and so forth.' Difficult for any of us, in this world, to say what we mean. Our friends, our keepers, are listening. Easier to see the world through our keepers' eyes than see for ourselves. Not just easier, safer. The elders might throw me out of the mosque: my husband might divorce me, my lover might leave me. Rushdie should die: I'm not a feminist.

Me, I blame no one. Who ever said life should be hard?

I wish someone, Christian or Muslim, would *define* this God they seem to share. Who is He? What is He? What offends Him? What pleases Him? Why did He make the world so troublesome? Why are we obliged to please Him? In case He herds us into Gehenna? What sort of morality is that? I am prepared to make my own definition of God – that is to say, the principle that I (this fictional 'I', remember) do not want to hear blasphemed. The God I recognise is the ordinary human capacity to feel joy and sorrow, hope and disappointment, in proper proportion; and without let or hindrance: a sense of the transcendent: if that is denied or insulted then, I must admit, I too begin to feel a deep grief and hurt, and know perfectly well what it means; and want to go to law and sue everyone in sight: though I still don't quite get to kill, kill, kill. These 'religious' emotions tend to be free-floating; they will attach themselves, as anxiety does, to whatever's around. They're powerful. I think it a pity when they attach themselves to the Koran, because I see it as a limited and limiting text when it comes to the comprehension of what I define as God. But then I would, wouldn't I? Look, you *can* build a decent society around the Bible: if you value the Gaia notions that pervade the Old Testament, puzzle over the parables of Jesus, argue about the Epistles, suspect the visions of St John the Divine; why, yes, reading all that and marvelling, you might just about have a blueprint for building heaven on earth. But the Koran? No. It doesn't acknowledge the concept. Heaven (or hell) is for hereafter: forget now.

Lately I saw a vaguely biblical musical put on by schoolchildren in the local cathedral; jolly prelates cycled over memorial slabs in the aisles in their attempts to popularise religion. I cannot believe the sacrifice of dignity is pleasing to the deity. But I was not afflicted by 'deep hurt and anger', not enough to cry 'kill, kill, kill!' But then, of course, being white, middle class and prosperous nothing deeply hurts me. I believe heaven is here on earth: it is, by the standards of most people in the world.

◇

Chatter, Chatter, Chatter

THIS NATION, this barely cohesive group of 60 million souls, striving for righteousness, is run, organised and governed by the likes of myself. We talk to each other on TV and in the newspapers; we have our conversations in public, on the radio: we make documentaries and political programmes and TV dramas for one another, casting a morning edition of the *Sun* in the direction of the masses, and an evening edition of 'Blind Date' likewise, as if we were feeding a pet cat, quietening its yowls, its passion to be heard. Our guilt is such that once we've coined useful phrases like 'deep hurt and anger' we believe them. Shocked out of slumber by the Rushdie Affair, still reeling, we mistake the symptom for the disease.

The upset, the affront, is not caused by a book, how could it be? It is caused by the awfulness of the society we have allowed to grow up around us; in which our brothers and sisters in God are obliged to dwell: in which bare bosoms wave from Page 3, gang rape oozes out of Winner's 'Death Wishes' 1

to 5, while rows of Cilla Blacks wave out of Radio
Rentals' windows at the derelict, drunken and devas-
tated who, homeless and foul smelling – if you're
homeless for more than three days, they say, you
smell of urine and sweat and only the really masochis-
tic will do anything for you – stare in at the moving
shadows at the back of Plato's cave: illusions of a
reality which is itself an illusion. And no one asks
them into the warm, or offers them the use of a tap.

So 'deep hurt and anger' becomes within a week a
weasel word: a phrase sucked of meaning. 'Kill,
kill, kill Rushdie' does not to me mean deep hurt
and anger at Rushdie, it means a plague on you and
all your works, on your rotten society: a society so
appalling even the rules for living and believing laid
down for hot-climate living by a sixth-century poet/
warrior/businessman living in a primitive and
largely illiterate society seem preferable to any you
lot – that's us lot – have to offer. A plague on your
folly, your arts, your alleged freedom of speech –
what about us?

Sackcloth and ashes.

A kamikaze attack: a suicide attempt: the familiar
'cry for help' – that innocent phrase used by those

who cling to life, who can't even begin to comprehend the despair of the oppressed, to those who'd really rather not have life at all. 'Mr Jones, Mr Jones, tell me. When you jumped off the bridge, was that a cry for help?' A cry for help, a spasm of fury, take your pick – on the part of those, who, like their white middle-class, well-intentioned oppressors, also do their best to understand and forgive.

My great complaint against the God of Islam, this God of vengeance, wrath and occasional forgiveness, who rules by terror and threat, is that the only human success he allows his followers is in *not* reaching their doubting, wondering, marvelling potential. A frustrating and maddening catch-22 here in the Koran. To be good, in the terms of the Prophet's instruction, is too often the exact opposite of being good in ordinary terms. To be good according to Mohammed is to chastise your wife and children when they're rebellious (as defined by the Prophet) – and you may take the hand of the unbeliever when he offers it to you, but when his back is turned the advice is to slay him. 'You have my full authority,' says the Prophet. The Koran looks harshly upon any twinge of doubt or disbelief; no crises of faith for them, no doubting bishops' 'Look here, do we really believe that Jesus went up to heaven in the *flesh*, or will just the spirit do?' It is in Christianity's permission to doubt, its ever-growing taste for parable – preacher's trick, Jesus' forte – which of late has developed into an appetite for fiction – for plays, novels, operas, more recently still film – these vigorous exercises in empathy, these passionate examples of alternative realities, that have permitted – encouraged, if you ask me – the West's progress out of savage barbarity in the name of God towards freedom of belief; out and away from the Crusades, leaving behind the killing and torture of religious dissenters, the intricate horrors of the Inquisition, the burning of witches, into our agreeable and passive over-tolerance of everything and anything, including Mr Murdoch's Page 3 girls. Nothing good without something bad. But the bad need not be permanent.

◇

Tee, Hee, Hee

TO SAY that Page 3 was responsible for the Rushdie affair may be going a little too far, but not all that far. I remember well the jeers of derision when Claire Short tried to put it to the House of Commons that perhaps human dignity was not well served by the appearance of these dehumanised breasts, appearing by the million at the nation's breakfast tables to British cries of 'What about her, then? Ooh, I'd like to get into that!': the tittering of children in the nation's classrooms (before or after the civic responsibility lesson? the sacrament that is sex, and all that junk) overcoming the reluctance of the boys and the uneasiness of the girls, as the female instinct to act with modesty and decorum in front of strange males is got the better of. Better surely to be unclothed in the privacy of your own home, and to some purpose, than prance thus naked, sealed for ever in masturbatory newsprint, wrapping up the fish and chips. The lewdness, the loucheness of the *Sun*'s Page 3 insults both men and women, boys and girls. Let those who jeered put on sackcloth and ashes: let them try and

17

dissuade the Muslim fundamentalists who look at our newspapers, at the *Sun*, at the *Sunday Sport*, and say 'So this is Western society!' and put their own women in total protective clothing. Let those jeering MPs find an answer to the Muslim women themselves, who claim to feel easier and safer thus unexposed, the males of the host society being so given to lascivious gawping, lewd remarks and rapes round corners. We British and our liking for Page 3 girls, above the waist okay, below not: flaccid penises allowed on film, erections never, female orgasm yes, male orgasm no – what does the Equal Opportunities Commission *do* all day? – find ourselves pitied and derided in the rest of Europe, where far stronger sexual and erotic images are freely available, but only to those who seek them out.

Sackcloth and ashes – what a seedy, shoddy way we have of going about these matters of sexual titillation.

'A plague upon your lewd habits!' cry the Muslims, burning Salman Rushdie's book. They should be burning Page 3, but they don't want to be jeered at either.

Sackcloth and ashes! Deep hurt and anger! Of course, of course. They speak for all of us. Kill,

kill, kill, to the tune of our vandal adolescents. 'If you love it, we will hate it: if you made it, we will break it. It wasn't what we wanted.'

Never what we wanted.

◇

We have backed ourselves into a peculiar corner in our attempt to be consistent: if we are to allow freedom of thought, we reason, if we are to allow *The Satanic Verses*, why then we must not interfere with the liberty of Mr Murdoch's male employees vilely to entertain other men at the expense of women and children. (I am not, by the way, taking time out to blame Mr Murdoch for anything. There are enough doing that already. He is what he is and can't help it. I blame those who let him get where he is, and those who *can* help it: those who write what they don't believe to be true, in return for the money he offers. To blame Mr Murdoch is like Adam blaming Eve. 'She offered me the apple. If she hadn't, I wouldn't have eaten it, would I? But, oh, the bitch, she tempted me!'.)
Oh paradox, paradox! Sackcloth and ashes. In the name of Freedom of Speech we permit what is seedy and disagreeable, and incites to rape. In order to maintain what is good we permit what is bad. We lose our greatest weapon: the superior virtue of our cause. Look round our city streets – see the TV

aerials sprout – and every one an incitement to lust, greed, violence, loutishness, ignorance – count up the hours – how much is 'good' TV? Very little. Mostly it's game shows, quizzes, adverts, pop groups, awful, awful films, fantasy deaths, trivial news – this is the world of the unbeliever. 'Ouch, that's elitism!' someone cries. 'Can't have that. No value judgements here, thank you. If the people want it, the people should have it.' And the good-natured and well-intentioned retreat, as if their tampering fingers have been burned. Can't have that. Stop this and we have to stop that. No 'Miami Vice' today means no editorial in the *Guardian* tomorrow. Let the children watch the despondencies of Taggart: real life's like that. Everyone knows. Rub their growing noses in the dirt. Of course they graffiti the walls. Who wouldn't? Why are we surprised? In the name of Freedom of Belief we dwell contentedly (or thought we did) in our multi-cultural, multi-religious society: it doesn't work, but who dares say so?

I do not believe it is beyond human ingenuity to restrain persons of low calibre who commit blasphemy against the God of my choice (the one, if you remember, who allows the human race to realise its sexual, emotional, rational and spiritual potential) whilst allowing, indeed encouraging, Salman Rushdie to speak in parables in His service.

Our censorship regulations for film and video are bizarre because they search – as do our criminal laws – for some rational system which can be economically enforced without anyone having to make a 'value' judgement – that is, say this is good, this is bad, this is simply horrid, this is horrid but interesting – (wow or yuk, in contemporary terms) – in areas of human response which are not rational.

Sackcloth and ashes, that in the real world we speak not what should be spoken; and in the world of fantasy speak what should be left unspoken.

Sackcloth and ashes.

◇

Every case, every film, is different. What is okay, what is not okay, depends upon context and intent. Children take the film classifications (at the moment U, PG, 15, 18) not as warnings, but as permissions. They wait to be 15, (or appear to be 15) in order to see the '15' film. 'Now I am old enough to swear at my mother. 18? At last, at last, grown-up enough to rape the girl next door!' (Do not believe young men identify with the terrors of the raped; they share the pleasure of the rapist. It is a real turn-on.) Watch any of Winner's 'Death

Wish' films – you who read this – go and see them. Perhaps film censorship, if censorship we have, should not be for the viewer, but imposed at the maker's end – as it is, most films are made to the extreme of sadistic violence, and edited down to the outer limit of what the censor permits in each category in each country. So many frames of raped flesh, so many frames of knives cutting breasts, so many frames of foaming blood, of tortured faces – or else let the whole thing go free, as many European countries do. Let those who need the fantasy-fodder for masturbation seek it out, and those who want to make it, make it: but let us not offer it to our young as their proper diet, as we do at the moment.

◇

Moo, Moo, Moo

WE'RE SCORNED for our ambiguities, our weaknesses, our worship of the sacred cow by the fundamentalist Muslims in our midst, and rightly. Look around, look around. The drunkards in the streets, the homeless, the purposelessness of our alienated youth, our gracious youths and tender girls turned white-faced, spotty, angry, dirty; our elderly confused, unhealthy, ignorant. Go into any doctor's waiting-room, any hospital casualty department or medical ward, and see what our society *does* to people. The NHS, oh sacred cow, oh cruel bitch, has in its forty years produced a very grisly and unhealthy race of medicine-addicted citizens. 'Our hospital', we are taught to say, as if 'hospital' was somehow part of our lives. 'Our NHS, a model for the world!' Oh Christ! Allah help the world, in that case. I get to see (for reasons which I shan't go into now but which cause me little pain and less distress, and which I do very little to cure because the workings of hospitals are so illuminating) the inside of many hospitals. From Helsinki to Auckland, with stops in Denmark, Germany,

23

France, Yugoslavia, Russia and New York on the way, I have put in my attendance in casualty departments, and nowhere, nowhere is there anywhere so awful as the Royal Free in Hampstead. Not because of the staff – who are as cheerful and efficient here as anywhere (my condition, being both dramatic and instantly curable with the help of a little advanced technology, brings out the best in them: and I would say that, wouldn't I, inasmuch as I'll probably find myself there again) – but because of the dirt which nobody cleans, the daubed walls which nobody paints, the blood-soaked rags in corners which nobody picks up, the waiting-room on a cold night filled with the destitute pretending pain or illness in order to get a bed for the night, harshly dealt with. 'First real patient we've had all night,' say the staff to me. 'The rest have been rubbish.' If you have to fake a pain to survive that pain is real enough. Let them in! Give them the mattress on the floor they need, the cups of tea they want. It isn't shortage of money which causes this epidemic of uncharity – what is money but a measure of labour, skill, resources? – it's our acceptance of ugliness; the plastic beaker that holds the tea lies where it falls. The Graces have fled.

Sackcloth and ashes, that we thus passionately defend this entity 'The NHS' without looking to see what it has done to us. And the alternative is not 'private' medicine, with its built-in incitement to keep patients ill, but some other structure, in which money is spent to keep us healthy, not cure our ailments. Mind you, the latter is more fun, provides more excitement, for those with a medical turn of mind. Those who exercise the healing skills like to have people to work upon, no doubt about it. They love drama, emergencies; that's why they do it.

In the Royal Free I understood sometimes why Allah is vengeful, despises the unbelievers. If I were him I'd slaughter the lot of us and start again. But why do his followers, then, pick on Mr Rushdie as if he were to blame for everything wrong in the world? Kill, kill, kill and then everything will be all right! Why, because someone must be to blame: we *have* to believe that God is good; when the going gets tough, when illness strikes, or impotence, or doubt, or the true Islamic state loses a war against the not so Islamic state next door, Iraq – why then, let's blame old Mother Shipton or Salman Rushdie. Understandable, but hardly forgiveable, and barely sensible. God bless the Royal Free. Someone has to.

In Helsinki General there wasn't much money and not much room, and the corridors were lined (as in St Thomas's, in St George's) with unconscious patients but not (as in St Thomas's, St George's) with patients waiting for beds, but with unconscious drunks, fully-clothed, booted feet dangling. In Helsinki hospitals every patient gets a blood test and the results of that blood test are patiently explained to every patient, peasant or lawyer: cholesterol levels, iron levels, white cell count – everything; so the patient can go away and look after himself. Everywhere but in Britain if you don't know your own blood pressure you're considered a fool. Our doctors like to keep it to themselves. Secret records. Insanity! And we let it go on.

In Yalta the legs of elderly Russians were in a much better state, less blotchy, less varicose-veined, more mobile at the knee and hip than the legs of a visiting party of tourists from the North of Britain. Mind you, animated chatter rose from the UK party; they twittered away like lively birds in spite of their legs: the Russians by comparison were glum and silent. The state of legs is not the only way to judge a society. You don't get a chance to see the legs of Islam, do you? Perhaps for good reason.

Sackcloth and ashes. We let it happen. Our sacred cow, the NHS, must be protected and stroked while it moos itself to death.

In Bath Royal United Hospital the casualty department fills up on a Sunday afternoon with giant laughing rugger players, bones sticking through brave flesh. They only play for the drama of the hospital. People drive recklessly in the expectation of ambulance rescue, hospital drama. I believe it. Well, some do. Remember the time the fire departments went on strike? Fires dropped by a third: or so Management claimed.

It is dangerous to say such things, I know, in case some Minister of the Crown seizes upon the notion of the less the better and cuts services still further. But that was never a good reason for not speaking the truth, was it – that it was dangerous? That it played into the hands of your enemies? Or was it?

Sackcloth and ashes! You can tell a nation by its hospitals. Ours are so dirty and mournful.

Sackcloth and ashes.

◇

Please, Sir, Sir, Sir –

SACKCLOTH AND ashes. Our educational system. My eleven-year-old son goes to a junior school, and a comparatively civilised one: there are thirty-three in his class and one teacher. He has a friend who goes to a state school in Munich. There are twenty-three children in that lad's class, and four teachers and one helper, and his mother is beside herself because there are so many children to so few staff. And we just tut and moan and let it drift on. Go to any big secondary school in Britain and you will find it full of children who don't want to be there, and bad-tempered teachers who believe it is ordinary and acceptable to insult their pupils. Forget policemen for the corridors, every school needs its own libel officer. How have these enormous unnatural units come about? Why do we snatch our children from their mothers and herd them together to bully and be bullied? Age, or lack of it, is not enough to ensure people get on together. Children are people too.

Our schools act as huge holding-pens for the young, the angry and the alienated. Why ever did we put the school leaving age up? What was the point? Why do our adolescents have to stay around to be insulted? To be sworn at, intimidated, jeered at, by exhausted and irritated teachers? If you don't believe this is how teachers behave, ask the children. Those who teach by vocation are few: those who end up teaching are many. Those who run our education departments sink into bureaucratic stupor, folly and resentment of change. The new Education Act can't be worse than what went before. Why do we fight it? It may not be too late for parents to take responsibility for their children back from the state: may not: though whilst education is compulsory it can only be an illusion that they do. And what is the point of this God of literacy, universal education, if it ends up with Page 3? Reared, educated, to read the *Sun*!

Of course Muslims want their own schools. They point to ours and say, 'What, have my sons, my daughters, grow up in the middle of all that profanity, that despair, that graffiti, that dinginess –' and they insist on their religious rights in this multi-cultural, multi-religious, benighted society of ours, and almost convince us, so great is our guilt, that they're right. Of course they're not right. You cannot, should not, teach a primitive, fear-ridden religion, beat it into children, as the lesser of two evils. There are other ways out. There must be.

Why can't we have compulsory schooling until, say, 11 – most children quite like primary schools: they're small, for one thing – then ten more years of it, out of taxes, at whatever stage of our lives we fancy? And if never, then never. What are machines for, but to liberate us from work? We must learn to value idleness. Let us do nothing, if that's what we want. Better to hang about street corners amiable, in dignity and from free choice, than to hang about them furious and despondent.

In the meantime, if I were faced with sending an eleven-year-old daughter into an inner-city comprehensive, 2,000 strong, with police patrols in the corridors, or into a school for Muslim girls, I might well be tempted to do the latter. I would not want her brutalised, coarsened. What alternatives are we offering our own Muslim population but a retreat into fundamentalism and kill, kill, kill?

And we have done nothing, nothing. Sackcloth and ashes.

◇

Bleat, Bleat, Bleat

IN CHILE, that Catholic land we see as the focus of cruel and fascist government, contraceptives were recently made free. The abortion rate dropped by a third. So did the birth rate. If we truly wanted a decent and civilised society we would stop bleating about the 'wrongness' of abortion, the detail of so many weeks allowed, so many not, and provide free contraception for everyone, male or female, what you want when you want. Forget 'encouraging promiscuity', that hark-back to days of yore, when fear of pregnancy kept girls chaste. Whether girls are chaste or not is their business: their getting pregnant ends up the state's business, since the state feels so obliged to 'educate' the child. More's the pity.

Sackcloth and ashes. Our attempt at multiculturalism has failed. The Rushdie Affair demonstrates it. The Bullock Report on Education, in its good-heartedness, led us astray in its yearning to voice a noble sentiment, to gain universal approval. Thus:

> No child should be expected to cast off the language and culture of the home as he/she crosses

the school threshold, nor to live and act as though school and home represent two totally separate and different cultures.

But they do, they do. How can we maintain the pretence that they do not? Of course there is racism in our schools, amongst our children, each group clinging to its own, disliking the other, if this nonsense is spoken, believed, fought for. The uniculturist policy of the United States *worked*, welding its new peoples, from every race, every nation, every belief, into a whole: let the child do what it wants at home; here in the school the one flag is saluted, the one God worshipped, the one nation acknowledged. Of course bad resulted as well – the terrifying insensate pride of the 'Americans', the concept of the American way of life, of 'American Freedom', have worked terrible evils in the world via the CIA – Vietnam, Nicaragua – but perhaps this time round we could get the benefits without the drawbacks? Our children would grow up with a sense of common identity – be they Afro-Caribbean, Asian or European in origin – not paralysed by confusion. Your God or mine? Your curry or my chips? Your sister on the hockey field, my brother down the mosque? No one ever prepared to say – or only the Muslim – our God is better than yours.

The paralysis of the well-intentioned! Who is there left of us brave enough to state what we believe? That, say, the Bible's a superior revelatory work to the Koran – or at any rate reveals a kinder, more interesting, less vengeful, less cruel God, one worth studying, worshipping? One who is not forever recommending Gehenna for unbelievers, forever threatening with eternal fires and roasting on iron hooks for anyone who transgresses His peculiar and idiosyncratic rules? One you can interpret? All you can do with the Koran is learn it by heart.

Oh, blame Rushdie, blame Rushdie, feel the 'deep hurt and anger' as belief is challenged: as the painful awareness of common sense begins to bite, as ideas flit to and fro on the radio everyone hears, on the TV everyone sees; ideas creeping in amongst the game shows, the quiz shows, the give-away shows, the cop shows, the dreary excitements of 'EastEnders', the awful machismo of 'Miami Vice' lookalikes, the general incitements to greed, violence, abuse, alienation, despair. Just the tiny trickle of ideas perhaps, but nevertheless thoughts, perceptions, an increasing understanding that perhaps Allah is not the one true God; or not in the sense He has been shown, not in the one learn-by-rote reality offered by the prophet Mohammed in the sixth century. And doubt is painful, belief is all you

33

have if you're the believer in the appalling world of the unbeliever; let's get Rushdie. Kill, kill, kill!

We should have listened sooner to what Rushdie was saying about our own society. We didn't. In *The Satanic Verses* Rushdie speaks truth in parable; he writes about the sickening racism of this country of ours, the dreadful indignities, the awful absurdities endured by our immigrant population, our 'ethnic minority' – which the best of us respect, if for the wrong reasons; and the worst of us persecute, kicking, spitting, deriding, often for good reason, as the two cultures clash and collide. Our National Front gangs Paki-bash, unable to distinguish colour of skin from religion, culture. We do nothing. Police brutality, police racism continues. 'Send them back where they belong.' We yawn. We do nothing. Only a novel.

Sackcloth and ashes.

◇

Oh Sister, Sister

SACKCLOTH AND ashes. The Feminists. Too involved in rooting out ideological heresies, most of us, to worry about the fate of the Muslim women in our midst, with their arranged marriages, their children in care, their high divorce rate: the wife-beatings, the intimidation, the penalties for recalcitrance: the unregulated work in Dickensian sweatshops, as, abandoned and betrayed, they try to keep house and home together: the impossibly exploitative piece-work at home because its imposs-ible to get out: – back to the days of *The Song of the Shirt*, 'with fingers weary and worn' – forget all this, ignore it, it's inconvenient; pleasanter, easier to be seen on the side of ethnic minorities, all in favour of the multi-cultural, too idle to sort out the re-ligious from the racial, from the political: too fright-ened of being labelled white racist, elitist, to interfere. Because the best have become frightened of labels: feel they must act and think together: are too frightened of the disapproval of their peers to speak the truth: too abandoned, for a full ten years, to a cosy general disapproval of anything, everything the current government does to be much use to anyone: slaves to liberal orthodoxy. And the black feminists, too put-upon by the black brothers, who insist that any white interference is by definition racist, the imposing of white middle-class standards upon ethnic working-class people, to dare say no, no, we are all sisters: our problems are the same. The greater racism, of course, is the blanket assumption which defines people by race and creed and not as individuals – but we have let ourselves be frightened by the labelling, the name-calling – racist, elitist, middle class – right out of the fray, and the religious extremists under this cover (I suspect forging this cover) have rushed in to take over. Burn Rushdie, kill Rushdie, provider of the Idea. Not one of them goes to prison for incitement to murder. No one dares enforce the law of the land. We're frightened, in the habit of being frightened.

Prison; now there's another story. Hang the head in shame.

Sackcloth and ashes.

◇

Write, Write, Write

WHEN *The Satanic Verses* won the novel category
of the Whitbread Prize, when it was just another
novel, not the centre of world events, I was prevailed
upon to speak at the prize-giving ceremony. I have
my notes. Herewith:

'Now Mr Rushdie's work and person,' I said, 'is
surrounded by controversy: his novels, as great
novels do, arouse hostility and unease as well as
passionate advocacy. There are some who wish he
would practise rather more economy of expression:
wish he would meet a modern equivalent of Ezra
Pound: let us not suppose these views were not
expressed at our (judges') meetings. But the vitality
of this magnificent book, its sheer ambition, its
arrogance, its way of sweeping continents and cultures together and waiting for the clash: linking
past and present, space and time, myth and what
we presume to call reality, within an English prose
we never knew could be so elastic, so elating defies
any but the most timid of souls *not* to give it a prize.
But the English literary establishment is not given
to sticking its neck out, is it: it is timid and nervous

37

of the new. It looks out for tricks. It is terrified of being conned. It finds it safer to sneer and jibe than accept what is new. I don't know what this establishment is, where it is to be found – it is just in the literary air; it is composed, I suppose, of critics, journalists, literary gossips, publishers – very seldom writers, or readers – those people who read books not to grind axes, but simply to enjoy them. I hope Mr Rushdie does not leave the country – as he is rumoured to be about to do – writers and readers here need him: his integrity and talent just might be infectious. In the meantime, I am told, *The Satanic Verses*, long though it is, heavy to pick up, is selling like the lightest and crispest of hot cakes. Of course it is. The public taste is not to be feared – it is our great defence.'

Well, well, so much for prophecy. The British Literary Community, which I was off-handedly accusing of a vague racism, has always suspected that Mr Rushdie was not 'one of us'. And that's true enough: he can stand on his head and outwrite most writers in this country, though his skin is darkish and his eyes are hooded and he was born in Bombay, albeit going to Rugby; and he does sometimes adopt a look of amused baffledom, appropriate enough in many of the circumstances in which in the past he has found himself but nevertheless unsettling; and certainly 'not one of

us' in his habit of taking upon himself extremes of
expression; permitting himself a breadth of thought
alien to those who specialise in searching for infinity
in a grain of sand or on an English beach on a wet
day; 'not one of us' in the sheer literary *chutzpah* of
what he takes upon himself to write; 'not one of us'
in his habit of issuing literary writs, as it were,
against the monstrously absurd; railing against
whole governments, nations, religions; against individuals who not only reflect a nation's anima, but
control that anima – the Virgin Ironpants in *Shame*,
Mrs Torture in *The Satanic Verses*. And of course
he is right: this is what happens, though we don't
want to believe it – *people* rule, not governments:
Caesar, Napoleon, Hitler, Nehru – and as for God
ruling, how do we know what He means? He can
only speak through such cracked human vessels.
Moses, Jesus, Mohammed – God may well be
speaking but He has only Mohammed's non-
celestial mind and being to filter the words through
– and we don't want to know it, no, we don't. What,
Mohammed sometimes got it wrong? Some verses
were indeed satanic? Give Rushdie the Whitbread
Novel-Category Prize? We can hardly not. It's a
literary prize. The Booker Prize? No. Too wild, too
uncontrolled for the coffee table: too much what
we don't want to know about ourselves – the magnificent, triumphant, glorious, mirthful eccentricity
of human society – let alone the confused nature

of the deity – and Rushdie is obliged to pay in person the consequence of both the corrupt barbarity of the capitalist West, and the anger and terror of the Muslim East at the moment of change, as the miserable rigour of the old ways begins to crumble and break. Not so much a sacrificial victim, perhaps, as an outcrop (if you like to see it like that) forced up by subterranean forces, round which the sacrificial dance is played. It must be terrifying to be so selected.

Odd that Arberry, the translator of the Penguin edition of the Koran, in the midst of his enthusiasm for the verses, complains of the repetitiveness and apparently random nature of many of its sections. 'Swinging from the steady march of straightforward narrative to the impetuous haste of ecstatic ejaculation,' writes Arberry of Mohammed. 'Sudden fluctuations of theme and mood!' he complains. The same charges, of course, as are laid against Rushdie's *The Satanic Verses*.

The understanding of fantasy as an alternative reality, of fiction as truth, of the poetic intuition which links them, is something that tends to escape the Brit. Lit. Comm. – the British Literary Community to you – who, as I say, from the beginning seem to have been baffled by the book and interpreted their baffledom by boredom.

'Didn't understand a word,' they claim. What does Arberry say? 'Attempting to measure an ocean of prophetic eloquence with a thimble of pedestrian analysis.' Oh yes. Sackcloth and ashes.

The Koran, that extraordinary piece of verse, gives the believer permission to hate the unbeliever. *The Satanic Verses*, that other extraordinary piece of poetry, does not, oddly enough, give permission to hate. It explains the nature of one culture in terms of the myths of the other: it exalts one and humbles another in unexpected places: the language of the mandarin and the colloquial collide as do mortal and immortal; archangel and whore; good and evil; the sacred and the profane. The collision strikes sparks; the sparks take fire: it is an advancement of the old theology: of course the world reels: it doesn't happen for no reason: this is the stuff of revelation, inspiration, the muse, call it what you like. It is commonly held to exist, have power: the idea taken form, shape, language. In fiction lies the religion, the spiritual advancement of the secular classes, in its low and high forms, exoteric, esoteric. It is how, at the exoteric level, we practise empathy, understanding, tolerance, standing in the other's shoes; how we, the non-believers, interpret Allah as compassionate, Allah as merciful: at the highest, esoteric level, where fiction drifts off and up into Literature, with its capital L, as the study of the

Koran drifts off and up into the highest realms of Sufi, towards mysticism, revelation, enlightenment. Literature in fact, as we see it in the Rushdie book, at the heart of the new humanist civilisation. Of course those of the dying world fight back. Kill, kill, kill!

Salman Rushdie, ex-colleague of mine in an advertising agency, is too humane, too modern, too witty, too intelligent, to lay down rules of conduct for the human race, let alone issue threats if they are not obeyed, but as a piece of revelatory writing *The Satanic Verses* reads pretty much to me like the works of St John the Divine at the end of our own Bible, left in, not without argument, by our own church elders, likewise made pretty doubtful by the contents. St Salman the Divine. Too far? Probably. But if into the weevily meal and the brackish water of our awful, awful society, this good yeast is dropped, and allowed to fizz and fizzle, froth and foam to good purpose, all may yet be well and our brave new God of individual conscience may yet arise.

◇

About the Author

FAY WELDON is one of Britain's foremost writers. Along with numerous television, radio and stage plays, she has written several highly successful novels – among them, *Down Among the Women* (1971), *Female Friends* (1975), *Praxis* – a Booker Prize Nomination – (1978), *Puffball* (1980), *The President's Child* (1982) and *The Life and Loves of a She-Devil* (1984; televised 1986).

CHATTO
CounterBlasts

Also available in bookshops now:-

No. 1 Jonathan Raban **God, Man & Mrs Thatcher**

No. 2 Paul Foot **Ireland: Why Britain Must Get Out**

No. 3 John Lloyd **A Rational Advance for the Labour Party**

Forthcoming Chatto Counter*Blasts*

No. 5 Marina Warner **Into the Dangerous World: Children and the Eighties**

No. 6 Mary Warnock **Universities: Knowing Our Minds**

No. 7 Sue Townsend **Mr Bevan's Dream**

Counter*Blasts* to be published in 1990 include:-

Tessa Blackstone on prisons and penal reform
Christopher Hitchens on the Monarchy
Margaret Drabble on property and mortgage tax relief
Ruth Rendell & Colin Ward on decentralising Britain
Ronald Dworkin on a Bill of Rights for Britain
Adam Mars-Jones on Venus Envy
Peter Fuller on the British Left

plus pamphlets from Michael Holroyd, Hanif Kureishi, Susannah Clapp and Michael Ignatieff

If you want to join in the debate, and if you want to know more about **Counter*Blasts***, the writers and the issues, then write to:

Random House UK Ltd, Freepost 5066, Dept MH, London WC1B 3BR